GRAMERCY GREAT MASTERS

Acknowledgments

The publishers would like to thank the museums for reproduction permission and in particular the **BRIDGEMAN ART LIBRARY** and **SCALA Istituto Fotografico Editoriale** for their help in supplying the illustrations for the book.

Louvre, Paris: Dante and Virgil in Hell; A Turk Smoking Sitting on a Sofa; The Death of Sardanapalus; Oil sketch for Sardanapalus; Sketch for The Death of Sardanapalus; Woman with White Stockings; Liberty Leading the People, July 28, 1830; (Portrait of) Frederic Chopin; The Taking of Constantinople by the Crusaders ; The Massacre at Chios; Women of Algiers in Their Apartment; Hunting the Tiger; Faust and Wagner in Conversation in the Countryside; A Turk Sitting; Hamlet and Horatio at the Graveyard; The Assassination of the Bishop of Liège; An Orphan at the Graveyard; The Death of Ophelia; Self-Portrait.

Musée d'Orsay, Paris: The Lion Hunt.

St. Sulpice, Paris: Heliodorus Driven from the Temple.

Musée des Beaux-Arts, Lyon: Woman with a Parrot.

Musée des Beaux-Arts, Nancy: The Battle of Nancy.

Musée des Beaux-Arts, Bordeaux: Greece Expiring on the Ruins of Missolonghi.

Musée des Beaux-Arts, Lille: Medea About to Kill Her Children.

Château de Versailles, France: The Battle of Taillebourg.

The Board of Trustees of the USA: The Shipwreck of Don Juan.

Wadsworth Atheneum, Connecticut: Turkish Women Bathing.

Hermitage, St. Petersburg: A Moroccan Saddling a Horse.

National Gallery, London: Ovid Among the Scythians; (Portrait of) Baron De Schwiter.

The Fine Art Society, London: Greeks Under Siege; Arab Horseman Giving a Signal.

Manchester City Art Gallery: The Natchez.

Fitzwilliam Museum, University of Cambridge: Odalisque.

Galleria degli Uffizi, Florence: Self-Portrait.

Ordrupgaardsamlingen, Copenhagen: (Portrait of) George Sand.

Credit Lauros-Giraudon: Jacob Wrestling with the Angel.

Christie's, London: Attila Followed by Barbarian Hordes Tramples Italy and the Arts; Orpheus Bringing Civilization.

Wallace Collection, London: The Execution of the Doge Marino Faliero; Faust and Mephistopheles.

Private Collection: Christ on the Cross.

Published by Gramercy Books
distributed by Random House Value Publishing, Inc.
40 Engelhard Avenue
Avenel, New Jersey 07001

Printed and bound in Italy

ISBN: 0-517-12403-3

10 9 8 7 6 5 4 3 2 1

Eugène Delacroix

GRAMERCY BOOKS

NEW YORK • AVENEL

Eugène Delacroix
His Life and Works

Delacroix was one of the most complex artists of his period, born into an age of fiery political passions, the turbulent epoch of France in the first half of the nineteenth century. During his lifetime, the First Republic and Napoleon's Empire gave way to the restored House of Bourbon. In turn, this was replaced by the Second Republic and then by the Second Empire. In his *Journal*, the diary that he kept during various periods of his life, Delacroix commented upon his many conflicts with the contemporary world. The commentary seems to show him suspended between the ideals of his personal and creative life and the reality of the powerful historical and social forces in turmoil around him:

"Absolute beauty is found but once, at a certain appointed moment in history. That makes it hard for the geniuses who follow. In periods of decadence there can be no hope of survival for particularly independent geniuses. They cannot lead the public back to the fine taste of ancient times, which would be understood by no one; but they can bring forth flashes that show us how they might have been in simpler times…. The arts have a childhood, maturity and senility. There are vigorous geniuses who come too early, there are those who come too late. Strange forces work both in one and the other. But like great minds in the times of decadence, even primitive ones fail to touch perfection."

Ferdinand-Victor-Eugène Delacroix was born on April 26, 1798, at Charenton-Saint-Maurice in France. He was the fourth child of Victoire Oeben, the daughter of a famous cabinetmaker for Louis XV, and Charles Delacroix, a minister under the Directory and later a prefect and ambassador of the Empire. It has often been claimed, however, on the basis of a certain physical

Greece Expiring
on the Ruins of Missolonghi
(detail)

resemblance and a series of telling coincidences, that his true father was Charles-Maurice de Talleyrand-Périgord — a cunning politician and diplomat who passed through political upheavals unscathed and occupied a prominent position through almost half a century of history, from the French Revolution and the Directory, to the Restoration, and even on into the reign of Louis Philippe. Yet Eugène himself never seems to have been perturbed by doubts about his paternity, and nurtured a strong admiration for his presumed father.

When Charles Delacroix died in 1805, young Eugène and his mother moved to Paris. There they lived with his sister Henriette, who was married to the ambassador Raymond De Verninac. At the age of ten, while studying at the Lycée Impérial, Delacroix was already a frequent visitor to the Louvre. During holidays in Normandy, at the country home of his cousin Nicolas-Auguste Bataille, he was fascinated by the mysteriously romantic atmosphere of the ruined abbey at Valmont and by the splendid medieval architecture of Rouen Cathedral. Both appear to have made a strong impression on his subsequent art.

The death of Delacroix's mother in 1814 plunged the boy into dire financial difficulties. However, a distant relative, Henri-François Riesener, himself an artist, managed to have Eugène taken on as an apprentice in the studio of the painter Pierre-Narcisse Guérin, a former pupil of Jacques-Louis David. Here, young Eugène met Théodore Géricault, for whom he posed as one of the figures in the celebrated *Raft of the Medusa*, first shown in 1819 at the Paris Salon, the annual exhibition organized by the French Academy. It was from Géricault that Delacroix learned to use color as an expression of the deepest and most irrepressible emotions of the human soul.

In 1857, remembering Géricault's art long after the painter's death, he wrote: "I see in it everything that David failed to achieve, the power of action, vigor and audacity." Géricault also encouraged Delacroix to make a closer study of nature and animals, particularly horses, a favorite subject for both artists. As Delacroix noted in his diary: "I really must start painting horses, and visit the stables every morning." Having completed his apprenticeship with Guérin, whose studio he continued to frequent for many years, Delacroix enrolled at the École des Beaux-Arts in 1817. The following year, the meager allowance that had been given to him by his relatives ceased, and he was forced to earn a living by painting the small portraits that gradually gained him a reputation.

Delacroix's first public commission came in 1819. This was *The Virgin of the Harvest*, a painting ordered for the parish church of Orcemont. That it was clearly inspired by Raphael's *Belle Jardinière* at the Louvre is quite understandable for a young painter who had just emerged from the intensely academic world of the École des Beaux-Arts.

In 1820, Géricault gave Delacroix a commission for an altarpiece, intended for a convent at Nantes, but now placed in Ajaccio Cathedral in Corsica. This *Virgin of the Sacred Heart* was strongly influenced by one of Michelangelo's sculptures, *The Bruges Madonna*. Later in the same year, Delacroix paid tribute to another of his ideal masters, Velazquez, in his *Self-Portrait as Hamlet*. In September he was taken ill with a mysterious fever, the first of many similar episodes of illness that would trouble him throughout his life.

In this period, Delacroix moved closer to the sphere of Romanticism, a movement that stressed personal expression and the world of feelings — in contrast to the formal rules and conventional portrayals of the Classical school. He read the works of Italian poets such as Dante, Petrarch and Tasso; and those of English authors, especially Shakespeare, from whom he translated several scenes of *Richard III*.

He also read the work of his own contemporary, Sir Walter Scott, without neglecting to build on the classical foundation that he had received at school.

Another commission arrived in 1821, once again from Géricault. This was for four semicircular canvases showing the personifications of the seasons intended as lunettes in the new dining room of the famous actor Talma. The style of these pictures lies somewhere between Pompeian wall paintings and the style of Michelangelo, revealing an artist still uncertain of his future direction, but nevertheless determined to continue with his experiments.

Delacroix's first important success came in 1822, with *Dante and Virgil in Hell*. Earlier, he had written to his friend Raymond Soulier that he intended to paint something for the forthcoming Salon in Paris: "… especially if it helps to make me better known. But at the moment I am so busy with other work that I doubt I can manage this, as so little time remains." Evidently this work was less demanding than expected, as Delacroix completed his painting and showed it at the Salon. This surprising masterpiece from such a relative beginner illustrates an episode from Dante's *Divine Comedy*, with the poet in the company of Virgil being ferried across the River Acheron by Charon. The painting reflects the attention that Romanticism devoted to the medieval period, which was seen as an age of free spirits and great minds expressing themselves powerfully. Dante, rediscovered after the oblivion of centuries, became one of the idealized heroes of the movement, but his original intentions were often distorted. Several episodes of the *Divine Comedy* were reinterpreted as the cry of rebellion of rational thinkers against the unfathomable mystery of the divine will and, more or less implicitly, against tyranny in any form.

Despite this brilliant opening, with all the hallmarks of Romanticism, Delacroix viewed the movement with a certain detachment. In his *Journal* he commented: "I am a pure Classicist," but then added that "if what is meant by Romanticism is the free expression of one's impressions, then I am a Romantic today, and was a Romantic even at the age of fifteen."

In its composition, the painting continues in the tradition of history painting dominated by David's followers, although there are also vague echoes of Michelangelo's *Last Judgment*. In its emotion, however, it is much nearer to the spirit of Géricault, while the power of the forms comes only from Delacroix, as does the handling of color. This follows the principle that an apparently monochromatic object can be constructed with vibrant juxtapositions of pure color, a technique that would later be pursued to its logical consequences by the Impressionists.

The painting met with a mixed reception. Many of David's pupils found it lacking in technical skill, and the critic Etienne Delécluze declared it to be "merely a shoddy daub." Nevertheless,

*An Orphan
at the Graveyard*
(detail)

14

other people understood the significance of the work, and two of these in particular would have a great influence on Delacroix's life and work.

Antoine-Jean Gros's *Napoleon Visiting the Plague-Stricken at Jaffa* of 1804, with its deeply tragic atmosphere and dramatic and livid colors, had made a profound impression on Delacroix. His admiration for Gros grew steadily, and years later he wrote: "Even after all the pictures I have seen, I find that his are still some of the worthiest in the history of painting." In 1822, however, Delacroix remarked rather ambiguously in his *Journal* that "Gros praised me with such indescribable warmth that I shall remain insensible to adulation for the rest of my life."

The journalist and critic Adolphe Thiers wrote in his newspaper *Constitutionnel* that "no other picture suggests a future as a great painter as does Delacroix's *Dante and Virgil in Hell*. Above all, here we can note that outburst of talent, that surge of superiority to come which rekindles the hopes that have been deluded by the excessive restraint of the other works." The article continued with allusions to the "boldness" of Michelangelo and the "exuberance" of Rubens. Thiers later embarked on a brilliant political career, and as Minister of Home Affairs under Louis Philippe he helped Delacroix to obtain a number of official commissions. Despite the heated discussion that Delacroix's *Dante and Virgil* provoked among the academics, it was greatly admired, particularly by his friend Géricault. Furthermore, it was purchased at once by Louis XVIII for the Musée Royal of the Palais du Luxembourg, a great compliment that must certainly have encouraged the young painter.

It was in 1822 that Delacroix started writing his aforementioned *Journal*, an extraordinary document that he continued intermittently throughout his life. This diary provides a vital key to Delacroix's character, recording his intuitions, disappointments, projects, and impressions, as well as anecdotes on the artistic circles of the time. It was written with a constant and vivid acuteness. Indeed, Delacroix once defined himself in a letter as "a savage contemplator of human nature."

Géricault died in 1824, a sad loss for Delacroix. At the Salon of that year Delacroix presented yet another provocative masterpiece, the *Massacre at Chios*, a moving depiction of a barbarous episode that had recently occurred in the war between Greece and Turkey. In the *Massacre* it is clear that Delacroix was by now devoting greater care to the backgrounds of his pictures, influenced by the landscapes of Constable which he had seen before they were displayed at the 1824 Salon. He had also read the works of Lord Byron, who had just died in the very same war. Also, Delacroix's presence in contemporary literary salons, where he met writers such as Stendhal, Mérimée, Humboldt, Hugo and Dumas, had brought him into contact with a realm of passionate discussion and political commitment. Consequently, in *Massacre at Chios*, the emotions and ideals that he had previously expressed only with themes from literature were represented as true life incidents and with deep compassion as a conscious participation in human suffering. The sober composition and subdued tones surprised those who had admired *Dante and Virgil in the Underworld*. However, the new simplicity of the figures, seen in totally different postures from the heroic poses preferred by David and his followers, showed Delacroix's profound sincerity. Despite the mixed reactions to *Massacre at Chios*, which was seen as an overt challenge to the academic traditions, it was purchased for the national collections. These paintings, intended as a form of political declaration, were only a part of Delacroix's overall activity. He worked frenetically on watercolor sketches, engravings, portraits and pictures with landscapes and animals; and he also wrote numerous articles and essays on art. Above all, he sifted through the classics of Romantic and medieval literature to discover new subjects to paint, creating interpretations that were rarely rhetorical and were often audaciously innovative.

During his long artistic career, Delacroix followed the vein of history painting with profitable results, and indeed, the dual themes of history and literature provided him with an inexhaustible source of inspiration. As he wrote in his *Journal*: "Everything is a subject, and the subject is you yourself, your impressions and emotions when faced with nature. You must look within yourself, and not about you."

Nevertheless, a distinct preference for scenes of violence seems to characterize Delacroix's output, episodes of horror

*The Assassination
of the Bishop of Liège*
(detail)

17

(Portrait of)
Baron De Schwiter
(detail)

18

that seem to delve deep into the murkiness of the human soul. This choice reflects a fascination for primitive sentiments that was common to much of the Romantic movement, and to the nineteenth century in general. Many of Delacroix's subjects can be interpreted in this light; from *Sabbath* (1824) to *The Execution of the Doge Marino Faliero* (1826), and from *The Assassination of the Bishop of Liège* (1829) to *Torquato Tasso in the Asylum* (1830). When Delacroix became a painter esteemed by even the highest echelons of society, it was historical scenes such as these that were most sought after by the aristocracy.

In 1825, Delacroix went to England with his friends Copley Fielding and Richard Bonington, whom he had known since the time of his apprenticeship in Guérin's studio. He visited the great museums of London and saw the work of the portrait painter Sir Thomas Lawrence; but his most important discoveries were the vivid landscapes of Constable and the vastness of Turner's skies. He returned to France with a renewed interest in watercolors, which he maintained for the rest of his life, often using the medium for animal subjects.

It is likely that in London Delacroix met Miss Dalton, a dancer with whom he maintained an affectionate relationship until 1830. His *Journal* in this period mentioned many fleeting romances and brief affairs, sometimes more imagined than real. Delacroix's greatest love was painting, and although he craved the warmth and delight of the senses that women could give him, his sentiments rapidly gave way to mistrust and discontent. It seems as if he could never dedicate to them the same intensity of passion that he reserved for his art.

Delacroix made yet another foray into the field of political commitment in 1826, with *Greece Expiring on the Ruins of Missolonghi*. Referring once again to the tragic war between Greece and Turkey, it was displayed at an exhibition organized by the French Romanticists in support of Greek independence. He also received a commission from the French government for a canvas showing *The Emperor Justinian*, but this was destroyed by fire in 1871.

Delacroix exhibited a total of eleven paintings at the 1827 Salon. These included *The Death of Sardanapalus*, inspired by an episode

A Turk Sitting
(detail)

20

from ancient history narrated by the Greek historian Diodorus — the collective suicide of King Sardanapalus of Nineveh and his concubines on a funeral pyre built with the immense riches of the royal palace. Despite the lavish Venetian mood of the colors and the spacious composition of the scene, the work was hotly disputed; the extravagant sensuality of the women facing their death with an air of almost voluptuary consent suggested an overwhelming atmosphere of overt eroticism. Delacroix lost much of his government support in the ensuing scandal, but in his *Journal* he recorded the incident with an unflinching sense of dignity. Viscount Rochefoucald, unofficially in charge of the fine arts for the nation, invited Delacroix courteously but firmly to "change style," whereupon the painter replied that this would be impossible, "even if the earth and stars should change their places." For several years after this scandal, Delacroix received only private commissions, and he turned to etchings as a way of making a living.

The July Revolution of 1830 and the installment of King Louis-Philippe by supporters of the House of Orléans provided the inspiration for the painting of *Liberty Leading the People*, presented at the Salon of 1831. Once again, Delacroix was strongly criticized for the audacity of his technique and the contents of his picture. The painting is a reconstruction of the three heroic days in which the Parisians erected barricades in the streets during their struggle against the reactionary and tyrannical government of Charles X, last of the Bourbon kings. Delacroix took no direct part in the uprising, but he roamed the streets of Paris collecting the visual evidence on which he later based his picture. The result was a skillful portrayal of the republican spirit of the French bourgeoisie, and it remains one of the most universally popular representations of the country's citizens and their desire for freedom. The new government purchased the painting, but it was relegated to the dark and inaccessible corridor of an anonymous ministry. Even with the change of regime, Delacroix was obviously considered too controversial a figure. This status was confirmed in November 1830 by his official exclusion from a competition held for decorations to be painted in the Chamber of Deputies.

In this period, Delacroix must have sensed that it was time for a change. Although his widespread literary studies continued to suggest possible subjects, the recent conclusion of the war in Greece had ended with the country's definitive independence from the Ottoman Empire. Further, the success of the July Revolution in France had perhaps deprived him of contemporary sources of inspiration. Despite his fall from official favor, he still had many influential friends in government spheres, and in 1832 they managed to have him included in a French delegation to the Sultan of Morocco.

The delegation sailed from the port of Toulon on January 10. After calling at Algeciras in southern Spain, where Delacroix noted that "everywhere around me is the throb of Goya," the party arrived in Tangiers on January 24. During his three months in North Africa, Delacroix traveled to Meknes and Algiers, with a brief visit to the Spanish port of Cadiz, but after an obligatory period of quarantine at Toulon, he was back in Paris on July 7. He filled seven albums with drawings and another with a series of eighteen watercolor sketches, which he gave to his friend and patron Count de Mornay. His artistic eye had absorbed sensations and scenes of penetrating violence; the opulence of African light and colors and the vivacious rites and customs of Arabian civilization had made an enormous impact on him. Every sight seen on his journey, every native gesture and every broad expanse of luminous landscape became a possible theme for a painting. In a letter to Auguste Jal, he wrote: "Beauty can be seen here by simply walking in the streets; one could go mad, and painting, or rather, the frenetic desire to paint, seems to be the most alluring form of madness."

His greatest single source of inspiration, however, was his visit in Algiers to the harem of a high-ranking captain of the Turkish governor, arranged in secret by local French officials. Delacroix was fascinated by the sweetly perfumed shadows of the harem, its sumptuous colors, clothes and fabrics — and above all, by the sultry beauty of its women, adorned in silks and gold, intent on their tasks of embroidery and weaving.

Many great masterpieces were born from the experience of this unforgettable journey. These included *Women of Algiers in Their*

*Hamlet and Horatio
at the Graveyard*
(detail)

23

(Portrait of)
George Sand
(detail)

24

Apartment (1834), *Jewish Wedding Feast in Morocco* (1837) and *Wading a Ford in Morocco*, painted many years later, in 1858.

When *Women of Algiers in Their Apartment* was presented at the 1834 Salon, its softly erotic atmosphere, warmly glowing colors and eloquently placid design were greeted enthusiastically by the public and critics alike. The novelist Théophile Gautier declared: "With its refinement and play of shadow and light, this picture is equal to the best works of Venice." Even Delacroix's former opponent Delécluze was forced to capitulate: "In this work there is such a distribution of light and a harmonious choice of tones, in the figures, draperies and objects, that we must acknowledge further qualities in the artist." Years later, in an article written for the 1846 Salon, Baudelaire commented: "This same melancholy wafts through *Women of Algiers*, Delacroix's most charming and flamboyant painting. This precious poem of an interior, brimming with repose and silence and full with splendid fabrics and ornate trinkets, emanates the heady perfume of a place of dubious repute that leads us towards unexplored regions."

Delacroix's return to Paris coincided with his definitive estrangement from the Romanticists. His *Journal* shows that he had the sensation of having arrived at a different form of maturity, transcending labels and trends to create his own style of pictorial freedom, and following only his personal tastes and ignoring the judgments of the critics. His circle of friends now included the writer George Sand and the pianist and composer Chopin, and he spent his time at concerts and musical soirées in preference to the literary salons that he had previously attended. He also started to visit the country home of the engraver Frédéric Villot at Champrosay, often to recover from attacks of ill health.

However, this new consciousness did not stop him from trying to gain commissions from the state again. Nor did it dissuade him from putting forward his candidacy for membership of the prestigious Institut de France, a privilege that despite repeated efforts was not granted to him until 1858. These contradictions are only superficial, however, for Delacroix's greatest desire was to know that his work would be protected in a way that only the constituted authorities could ensure. In 1833, after overcoming considerable resistance from other members of the government, the former journalist Adolphe Thiers managed to obtain a commission for his friend Delacroix. This vast cycle of decorations in the Salon du Roi at Palais-Bourbon kept Delacroix busy until 1838. He painted canvases in a distinctly Renaissance style for eight ceiling panels and four friezes above the doorways. These were divided into four principal areas dedicated to allegories of what he saw as being the supporting pillars of the modern state: *Justice*, *Agriculture*, *Industry* and *War*.

Although the results were greatly admired by critics and by the general public, Thiers had considerable difficulty in having another commission granted to Delacroix. Yet this came finally in 1840. This time it was the ceiling of the library of the same Palais-Bourbon that was to be decorated with mythological, historical and literary subjects. The immense project required years of preparation, mainly on account of the tremendous complexity of the intricate symbolic scheme that had to be devised. Delacroix worked some ten years on the decoration, helped by his pupils Lassalle-Bordes and de Planet.

For the two semicircular end sections of the ceiling, Delacroix painted *Orpheus Teaching the Greeks the Art of Peace*, contrasted by *Attila Followed by Barbarian Hordes Tramples Italy and the Arts*. The conflict represented is plain to see — peace opposed by war, the vital pulse of life opposed by death and senseless destruction. The five cupolas between these two semicircles are occupied by the *Sciences* (Pliny the Elder, Aristotle, Hippocrates and Archimedes), *Philosophy* (Herodotus, the Chaldeans, Seneca and Socrates), *Legislation* (Numa Pompilius, Lycurgus, Cicero and Demosthenes), *Theology* (Adam and Eve, the Exile in Babylon, the Beheading of John the Baptist and the Tribute of St. Peter) and *Poetry* (Homer, Ovid, Achilles and Hesiod).

This massive work, completed in 1847, proved to be a great success with the critics. In September 1863, shortly after Delacroix's death, Saint-Victor declared in *La Presse*: "The most important work by Delacroix is the decoration of the library at Palais-Bourbon.... A miraculous clarity dominates this profusion of episodes and images, the underlying thoughts are made clear by the forms.... And what admirable comprehension of Greek lucidity, Latin composure and Oriental sinuosity.... Delacroix made history come alive." Many modern critics, however, find Delacroix's creative flair and impetuous coloring severely cramped by the complex symbolism dictated by the subjects chosen, bringing an uncomfortable touch of heaviness to the swift and instinctive hand of a gifted artist.

The impressive cycle of decorations set the seal of approval on Delacroix's reputation with the French ruling classes. Thus in 1850 he was entrusted with the completion of a fresco on the ceiling of the Galerie d'Apollon in the Louvre. The work had been started some two centuries previously by Charles Lebrun, one of the founders of the French Academy of Painting and Sculpture and its earliest director, in 1683. The painting shows Apollo triumphing over the forces of evil, personified by the dying serpent Python, and the scene represents the violent conflict between the light of Reason and Civilization and the shadows of Chaos and Oblivion. The magnificent warmth of the colors, the strength of design and the captivating three-dimensional spaciousness of the work recall instantly the monumental splendors of Venetian and Baroque masters such as Veronese, Tiepolo, Titian and Rubens. In this work Delacroix returned to the artists that first inspired him, in a stupendous achievement that greatly pleased the critics of the time and still fascinates the viewer. The key to this vibrant scene lies once again in its skillful use of color, knowingly calculated and applied with the sensitivity that only a genius with a high level of technical competence could achieve.

Another example of this aspect of Delacroix's genius can be found in his preparatory notes of 1856 for *Medea About to Kill Her Children*: "Local colors of the large child in the second Medea: brown, red and white. These are softened as they meet the warm shades of the shadows, slightly orange when the lighter tones are mixed with green, pink, yellow and white. Light colors of Medea, her cheeks, breast, torso, etc., are based on umber, white and yellow lake with white and lake." He continued by giving a detailed explanation of the best way to obtain the correct coloring for "the cheeks of a young and darkly-complexioned girl."

Delacroix's popularity was by now so great that at the 1855 Exposition Universelle in Paris a retrospective exhibition was organized in his honor. A remarkable total of forty-two works were shown, demonstrating that his success in establishment circles and with the public in general was firmly consolidated. This led to other official commissions of varying importance, and he worked on these while continuing to display regularly at the Salon exhibitions. However, the greatest challenge of this last period of his career was the painting of a series of frescoes for the ceiling and walls of the church of Saint-Sulpice in Paris, a project that occupied Delacroix from about 1850 until shortly before his death. Although he was an essentially atheist painter, Delacroix managed to endow the sacred subjects with a profound sense of religion that sprung from his sincere love for all aspects of life, even the most elusive and mysterious.

In his last years, Delacroix became increasingly indifferent to the clamor of public acclaim and the favors of the critics, led by such personalities as Charles Baudelaire, Théophile Gautier and the Goncourt brothers. His declining health and the loss of many of his closest friends and relatives caused him to withdraw almost totally into his art. To this he dedicated his greatest energies and unlimited love till the very end. Clasping firmly the hand of Jenny Le Goillou, his housekeeper and constant companion for almost thirty years, Delacroix died in his Paris home on August 13, 1863, a victim of the tuberculous laryngitis from which he had suffered since his early youth. At his funeral, a crown of gold was placed upon his coffin.

In the last pages of his *Journal*, Delacroix described his complex relationship with his art: "I have been painting all day; what a blissful life! The celestial reward for my so-called isolation…. To tell the truth, painting is almost a torture for me, it torments me in a thousand ways like a tireless and demanding lover. For the last four months, I have been up at dawn, and I run to this fascinating task as I would rush to the feet of my dearest mistress…. But from where does this eternal conflict come, this conflict that instead of dousing my spirits gives me new hope, that instead of discouraging me consoles, and when I have finally left it still occupies all my time? A fortunate reward for what the years have taken from me, a noble use of these instants of old age, which already besets me from a thousand different directions."

The Death of Ophelia
(detail)

Much can be said of the legacy that Delacroix left to his century and of his greater contribution to the culture of mankind at large. At times, he was revolutionary in his experiments, at others he was cautiously critical. His approach to art and to history never resulted in the sacrifice of the coherence that was essential to his work, and he refused to allow his many conflicts with the critics or the protection of his influential friends to separate him from his "tireless and demanding lover." The lesson that Delacroix teaches is one of honesty in a deeply felt calling, a burning love for art and a sincere closeness to his fellow men and the complexities of the human soul. Perhaps the warmest and most fitting tribute to Delacroix was that paid by Charles Baudelaire, writing in 1855:

"What will Delacroix be for posterity? What will this righter of wrongs say of him? It is already easy, given the point at which his career has arrived, to answer with little fear of contradiction. Like us, posterity will say that he was a single amalgam of the most stupendous abilities. That like Rembrandt he had a sense of intimacy and profound magic, that he had the flair for combination and decoration of Rubens and Lebrun, the bewitching colors of Veronese, and so forth. But also that he had an incomparable and indefinable quality that managed to reveal the most melancholic and passionate part of the century, a completely new talent that made him a unique and unprecedented artist."

Self-Portrait

The Massacre at Chios

The Massacre at Chios (detail)

Dante and Virgil in Hell

Dante and Virgil in Hell (detail)

The Natchez

Greeks Under Siege

A Turk Smoking Sitting on a Sofa

Odalisque

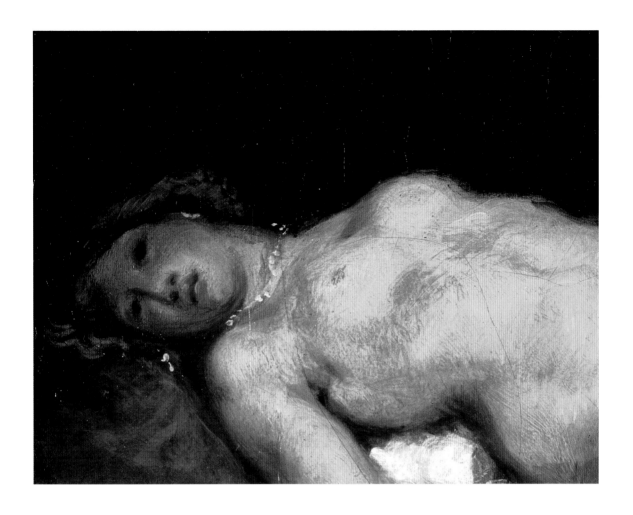

Odalisque (detail)

The Execution of the Doge Marino Faliero

The Execution of the Doge Marino Faliero (detail)

Faust and Wagner in Conversation in the Countryside

Faust and Mephistopheles

Sketch for *The Death of Sardanapalus*

Oil sketch for *The Death of Sardanapalus*

The Death of Sardanapalus

The Death of Sardanapalus (detail)

Woman with a Parrot

Liberty Leading the People, July 28, 1830

Liberty Leading the People, July 28, 1830 (detail)

Woman with White Stockings

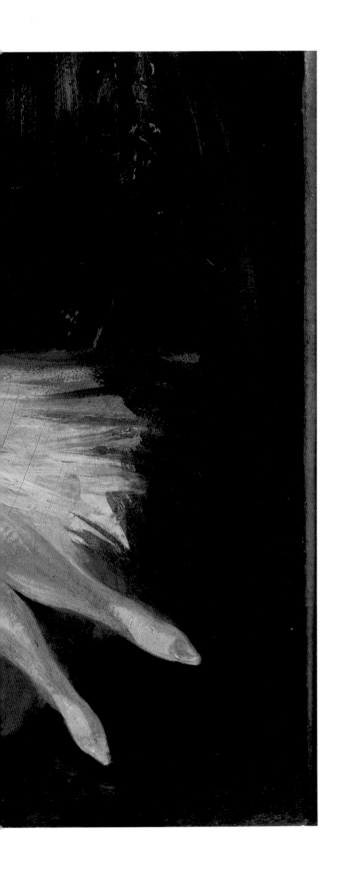

The Battle of Nancy

Women of Algiers in Their Apartment

Women of Algiers in Their Apartment (detail)

The Battle of Taillebourg

Arab Horseman Giving a Signal

Medea About to Kill Her Children

(Portrait of) Frederic Chopin

Self-Portrait

The Shipwreck of Don Juan

The Taking of Constantinople by the Crusaders

Attila Followed by Barbarian Hordes Tramples Italy and the Arts

Orpheus Bringing Civilization

Ovid Among the Scythians

Christ on the Cross

Jacob Wrestling with the Angel

Jacob Wrestling with the Angel (detail)

Heliodorus Driven from the Temple

Turkish Women Bathing

The Lion Hunt

Hunting the Tiger

A Moroccan Saddling a Horse